I have always loved to cook but baking is my passion. When I bought the Kettledrum in July 2005, I realised my aim to have my own café/bistro where fresh home cooked food and baking would be available all year round.

The Kettledrum has been in existence since the early 1900's and many customers tell of fond memories of the Kettledrum as first an Ice cream parlour and latterly a great café and bistro.

My collection of recipes in this book are from the Kettledrum and outside catering menus.

Although my catering days are now limited, and the Kettledrum cafe now leased; this book allows me to share my recipes far and wide.

I hope you enjoy them as much as my customers!

Patricia Lyon

Contents

Lentil or Pea & Ham Soup

Proportions: 50g lentils or green split peas / 1 litre water

1 ham shank
6 litres water or 6 litres ham bouillon if using stock cubes
300g lentils or green split peas
3 medium potatoes
3 large carrots
3 slices smoky bacon – cut into small pieces
Salt & pepper

1. Put everything in a pot and bring to the boil.
2. Simmer until lentils are soft.
3. Remove ham shank.
4. Blitz soup with hand blender.
5. Add water if soup very thick.
6. Taste. Adjust seasoning if more required.
7. This soup is best made the day before.
8. If re-heating – soup may have thickened and need diluting with ham stock.

PEA & HAM SOUP – substitute lentils with green split peas.

Cream of Vegetable Soups

Virtually any vegetable can be chosen as the main ingredient eg. broccoli cauliflower, celery, carrot & coriander etc.

Choose your main vegetable then make with base ingredients to create your s

Broccoli – 2 large heads
Or Cauliflower – 2 heads
Or Carrot & coriander – 6 large carrots, large bunch of coriander

Base
6 litres vegetable stock
2 large potatoes
Salt & pepper
250ml Double cream

1.   Put the base ingredients in a large pot with your chosen main vegeta
2.   Simmer until all vegetables are soft.
3.   Blitz with hand blender or in a food processor.
4.   Stir in double cream.

Check seasoning and add more salt & pepper if necessary.

Chicken or Ham Broth

6 litres chicken or ham stock
3 potatoes finely diced
3 carrots finely diced
1 celery stick finely chopped
500g broth mix
Sprinkle of mixed herbs
2 cooked chicken fillets or 4 slices cooked ham and 3 rashers smoky bacon finely chopped
Salt & pepper

1.   Put everything in large pot and simmer until all the pulses and vegetables are tender. About one and a half hours.

Check seasoning before serving.

Potato & Leek Soup

5 litres vegetable stock
6 large potatoes
4 leeks
Salt & pepper

1.   Peel and dice potatoes.
2.   Add to stock and simmer until tender.
3.   Chop leeks including green leaves.
4.   Add to soup 10 mins before serving.
5.   Season to taste.

Add a little milk or double cream if liked.

Chicken Liver Pâté

Serv

8 chicken livers – washed and any bile sacs removed
1 small onion
1 clove garlic
2 tablespoons brandy

1. Sauté livers, onion and garlic in olive oil until livers are browned and onion is soft. Add salt & pepper.
2. Add 50ml chicken stock and deglaze pan.
3. Leave to cool slightly then put contents of pan into food processor along with brandy.
4. Blitz until very smooth.
5. Spoon into individual dishes or into one larger dish.
6. Cool, then cover with clingfilm and refrigerate.

Serve with oatcakes.

Smoked Salmon & Prawn Rolls

Serve

4 slices Scottish smoked salmon
200g prawns
4 tablespoons mayonnaise
Dash of Tabasco

1. Make prawn cream – put mayonnaise, prawns and Tabasco with a li salt & pepper into blender. Blitz until smooth.
2. Lay salmon slices on board.
3. Spread layer of prawn cream over salmon slice.
4. Roll up each salmon slice and trim edges.

Serve with fresh green salad, lemon wedge and buttered brown bread.

Mushroom Ragout

Serves 4

2 double handfuls of mushrooms – cleaned and sliced
1 large onion – finely chopped
1 clove garlic – finely chopped
2 tablespoons vegetable stock
200ml double cream

1. Sauté mushrooms, onion and garlic until soft.
2. Add stock and simmer until stock reduces to virtually nothing.
3. Add cream, bring to boil and simmer until cream has reduced to thick sauce.

Serving suggestions:

1. Toast and butter two pieces of crusty bread. Pour ragout over toast and garnish with flat leaf parsley. Enjoy with large green salad.
2. Bake off large pastry case by cutting 4" square piece of puff pastry, marking circle in centre and baking at 220ºC/Gas 7 for 12 minutes. Fill with ragout and serve with selection of seasonal vegetables.

Steak Pie

1 kg shoulder steak - diced
1 large onion- finely chopped
2 tablespoons plain flour
2 bay leaves
2 oxo cubes
1 tablespoon tomato purée
Salt & pepper
1 litre water
1 packet frozen puff pastry

1. Fry diced steak and onions in oil until browned.
2. Add flour and crumbled oxo cubes. Cook for 1 min, stirring all the time.
3. Add salt & pepper, bay leaves, tomato purée and water.
4. Simmer for 1 hour.
5. Roll out pastry and cut into 3" squares.
6. Bake in hot oven for approx 12 minutes.

Serve each piece of puff pastry with a portion of cooked steak pie filling.

Lasagne

Serves 4

Oven 160ºC/ Gas 4
Approx 16 sheets pasta

Bolognese sauce

200g lean minced beef	2 rashers smoky bacon – finely chopped
1 onion – finely chopped	1 teasp dried basil
1 clove garlic – crushed	200g tin chopped tomatoes
4 tablespoons red wine	2 tablespoons tomato purée
Salt & pepper	

1. Using a thick based pot or pan, fry off the mince, bacon onion and garlic until browned.
2. Add tomatoes and purée, wine and seasoning.
3. Cover with lid and simmer for 20 minutes then remove lid and simmer for another 20 minutes until sauce is reduced.

White sauce

75g butter	50g plain flour
800ml milk	200ml double cream
Salt & pepper	Grated nutmeg

1. Melt butter into flour and cook for 1 minute.
2. Gradually add milk, stirring continuously. Bring to the boil and simmer for 3 minutes.
3. Stir in the double cream and 1 teaspoon grated nutmeg.

1. In a small roasting tin or dish make up the lasagne by layering first the Bolognese sauce and then the cream sauce with sheets of pasta.
2. End with a cream sauce layer.
3. Bake in oven for 40 minutes until pasta is cooked.

Alternatively: Add 2 oz grated cheese to the white sauce for a richer flavour.

Mince & Tatties

Serves 6

500g minced beef
1 large onion
2 tablespoons plain flour
2 oxo cubes
2 bay leaves
6-8 large potatoes, boiled and mashed

1. Brown mince with onion in heavy bottomed pot.
2. Add flour and oxo cubes and mix in well.
3. Cover with boiling water, add bay leaves, salt & pepper and simmer for 30 minutes.

Serve with mashed potato and garden peas.

Coronation Chicken

Use as a sandwich filling or in salads and baked potatoes.

2 cooked chicken fillets – chopped finely
4 tablespoons good quality mayonnaise
1 teaspoon madras curry powder
1 level teaspoon dried mint

1. Mix altogether.
2. Mixture will initially be pale but golden colour develops as madras powder infuses.

Chicken Curry

Serves 4

1kg chicken fillets diced
400g chopped onion
Ghee for frying (but oil will do)
2 crushed garlic cloves
1 teaspoon ginger
1/2 teaspoon English mustard
4 cloves
1 teaspoon cumin seed
1/2 teaspoon turmeric
1 heaped teaspoon chilli powder

Spice Bag
2 cardamom pods
2 inch piece of cinnamon bark

1 tin chopped tomatoes
1 heaped tablespoon tomato purée
1 teaspoon sugar
275ml water
2 tablespoons garam masala
1 tablespoon lemon juice

1. Sauté onion, garlic and ginger in the ghee or oil until soft.
2. Add all the spices and cook for at least 10 minutes.
3. Add the sugar, tomatoes, purée, water and bag of spices.
4. Cook for about 30 minutes until sauce thickens and reduces slightly.
5. Add cubed chicken and cook for 30-40 minutes.
6. Sprinkle the garam masala and lemon juice over the curry.

Check the sauce for taste, remove spice bag.

Chicken, Leek, Mushroom & Tarragon Pi

3 large cooked chicken breasts
2 leeks
8 large mushrooms
2 cloves garlic
1 dessertspoon tarragon

Serves

Sauce
30g margarine
1 tablespoon plain flour
250ml chicken stock
2 teaspoons mustard
1 teaspoon lemon juice
3 tablespoons double cream
Salt & pepper

1. Chop leeks, mushrooms and garlic and sauté in pan until soft.
2. Make sauce by melting the margarine with the flour and seasoning
3. Gradually add the stock and when it starts to thicken, cook for 1 minu
4. Add sautéed mixture along with chicken, herbs and double cream.
5. Put in ovenproof dish.
6. Roll out puff pastry and cover top of dish.

Bake at 220ºC/Gas 7 for 15 – 20 mins until golden brown.

Fish Pie

Serves 4

This is one of our most popular dishes

2 smoked haddock fillets
1 salmon fillet
570ml milk
Dill or mixed herbs
Pepper
6 medium potatoes – boiled and mashed

(Alternatively ask your fishmonger for smoked fish ends and salmon ends which are a fraction of the price.)

1. Put haddock, salmon, herbs and milk in a pot and bring to the boil.
2. Simmer for 5 minutes.
3. Flake fish in the pot with a spoon or knife.
4. Mix cornflour with a little milk and add to the fish pot.
5. Stir over heat until sauce thickens.
6. Season well – not too much salt as smoked fish is quite salty.
7. Pour into ovenproof dish then cover with mashed potato.
8. Crisp top in the oven for 20 minutes or under the grill for 4 minutes.

This dish improves with time so make the day before and reheat for 40 mins at 180ºC. Cheese can be sprinkled over the top if liked.

Green Herb Oil

Use this over salad leaves or to finish off a plate as part of the garnish.

Large bunch of herb leaves of your choice
2 cloves garlic
1 tablespoon Dijon mustard
1 tablespoon capers
200ml extra virgin olive oil
Salt & pepper

1.   Put all ingredients, except the oil, in a food processor.
2.   Add a little oil then run machine.
3.   Slowly pour in oil through spout. Stop processing and scrape sides
      then start machine again.
4.   Process until herbs are finely chopped and will pour from a
      squeezy bottle.

Uses :

Tarragon Oil – garnish chicken dishes.
Dill oil – garnish salmon or fish dishes.
Mixed herb oil – use as green salad dressing.

Spicy Onions

2 onions finely chopped
Tomato ketchup
2 teaspoons chilli
2 teaspoons mint

1.   Mix everything together using enough ketchup to give a
         dropping consistency.

Use as an accompaniment for filled rolls, salads, ciabatta grills.

Prawn Marie Rose Sauce

Use with prawn cocktail or prawn sandwich filling.

200g good quality mayonnaise
3 tablespoons tomato ketchup
Dash Tabasco sauce
1 tablespoon double cream

1. Mix everything together until smooth.

Luxury Chocolate Sauce

Serve over ice cream

750g plain chocolate
50g butter
135ml water
135ml golden syrup
3 teaspoons vanilla essence

1.   Break chocolate into small pieces. Add butter, water and syrup.
2.   Melt over hot water or microwave until chocolate melted.
3.   Add vanilla essence.

Brandy Butter

Perfect with Christmas pudding. This recipe brings back childhood memories as my mum made it every year. Add more brandy if liked.

200g icing sugar
100g unsalted butter
2 tablespoons brandy

1.   Cream all ingredients together until white.

Fill a fancy bowl ready for serving.

Butterscotch Sauce

This is our sticky toffee pudding sauce and has to be tasted to be believed. Can also be served with ice cream, other sponge puddings or any sweet dish. Make plenty as everyone will want more.

560ml double cream
150g margarine
300g soft light brown sugar
2 teaspoons vanilla essence

1. Place all ingredients, except the essence, in a saucepan over a medium heat. Stir until sugar is dissolved.
2. Boil for 2 minutes.
3. Stir in vanilla essence.

When cool store in fridge.

Truffle Icing

This is a rich icing suitable for adding a sumptuous dimension to cakes.

675g dark chocolate
850ml double cream

1. Heat the cream to just below boiling point.
2. Add chocolate and stir until the chocolate has melted into the cream.

Allow to cool slightly and when the mixture is thick enough , ice the cake.

Real Apple Pie

Tinned apples can be used but are never the same as fresh. I use golden delicio
as they keep their shape better and are a similar price to cooking apples. If
using cooking apples add some sugar.

8 inch (20cm) loose bottomed flan tin

1 quantity of biscuit crust pastry (see page 24)
12 golden delicious apples
1 tablespoon caster sugar
Cinnamon if liked

Oven: 160°C/Gas 4

1.	Roll out two thirds of pastry and line flan tin.
2.	Prick base and bake blind for 15 minutes.
3.	Peel, core and slice apples.
4.	Put in pot with sugar and cinnamon and a little water.
5.	Bring to boil and simmer for 5 minutes.
6.	Drain any excess liquid.
7.	Fill pie base with apple.
8.	Roll out remainder of pastry and cover top of pie.
9.	Bake for 40 – 60 minutes until golden brown.

Dredge with caster sugar.

Sticky Toffee Pudding

Serves 6-8

This is one of the Kettledrum's signature dishes.
Each day it gets stickier and stickier – if it lasts that long!

1x 4lb cake tin – greased and lined (the quantity will seem small but will rise significantly)
175g dates – stoned and chopped
350ml water
1 tablespoon bicarbonate of soda
50g margarine
170g caster sugar
2 medium eggs, beaten
175g self raising flour
1 teaspoon vanilla essence
1 portion of Kettledrum butterscotch sauce (see page 19)

Oven 180°C/Gas 4

1. Boil dates in the water for about 5 minutes.
2. Cream margarine and sugar.
3. Add eggs and beat well.
4. Add water and dates along with flour and vanilla essence.
5. Pour into baking tin.
6. Bake for 30-40 minutes.
7. Cool before turning out.
8. Make butterscotch sauce.
9. To serve – place slice of pudding on plate and put spoonful of butterscotch sauce on top. Microwave for 10 seconds.

Serve with custard, cream or ice cream.

Tiramisu

This is an authentic Italian Tiramisu which literally translates to 'pick me up'. Daniela, my friend, lives in Rome and showed me the method. It uses raw eggs so do not serve to the very young or very old.

6 eggs – separated
450g mascarpone cheese
150g caster sugar
300g savoiardi (Italian sponge fingers) biscuits
500ml whipped double cream
Strong milky coffee – to dip biscuits
Alcohol if wished (such as marsala or brandy)

1.   Beat egg yolks, sugar and mascarpone to a smooth cream.
2.   In a separate bowl, whisk egg whites until stiff then beat into cream
3.   Using a large serving bowl, layer by dipping biscuits into coffee mix
      and alternately layering with cream. Add alcohol to coffee mix if
      wished. Finish with a cream layer.
4.   Sprinkle cocoa powder on top to seal and decorate.

Refrigerate until set.

Brandy Snap Basket with Ice Cream

I use bought in baskets for this dessert.

1 shop bought brandy snap basket
1 scoop vanilla ice cream
1 dessertspoon butterscotch sauce
Drizzle of chocolate sauce

1.	Place spoonful of butterscotch sauce on serving plate and microwave for 10 seconds.
2.	Put basket on top of sauce and place a scoop of ice-cream into basket.

Drizzle with chocolate sauce before serving.

Biscuit Crust Pastry

This is a sweet version of shortcrust pastry and I use it for all tarts and pies with sweet fillings.

200g plain flour
Pinch salt
50g margarine
50g lard
2 dessertspoons caster sugar
1 egg yolk

1.   Place dry ingredients in mixer bowl.
2.   Add fats and mix until resembles fine breadcrumbs.
3.   Add egg yolk and enough cold water to bring mixture together to form pastry.

Rest for 30 mins before using.

Choux Pastry

70g plain flour
25g margarine
Pinch salt
2 small eggs
125ml water

1. Bring water and margarine to the boil.
2. Sift flour and salt onto a sheet of parchment paper and add to the boiling liquid.
3. Beat well until smooth and cook for 1 minute.
4. Allow to cool slightly then add eggs gradually, beating well between each addition.

For choux buns spoon mixture onto parchment paper and bake for 15-20 mins.

For eclairs – fill piping bag with large nozzle. Pipe 10cm strips and bake for 20 mins. When cooked, pierce with a knife to release steam then put back in oven for 4 mins to dry. When cool, fill with piped cream and coat top with melted chocolate or spoon over chocolate sauce.

Shortbread

Makes approx 24. I always use a mixer as it keeps everything cool.

200g caster sugar
400g margarine or butter
200g cornflour
400g plain flour
Half teaspoon salt

Oven : 180ºC/Gas 5

1. Cream margarine and sugar until white, light & fluffy.
2. Add salt, cornflour and plain flour. Run at low speed until all combine then keep mixing until mixture leaves side of bowl and comes togeth
3. Roll out on floured work surface until 1 cm thick.
4. Use a medium round cutter to cut biscuits.

Bake until just golden - about 20 minutes.

Empire Biscuits

1 batch of shortbread biscuits.   Strawberry jam
200g icing sugar   Glacé cherries

1. Sandwich two biscuits together with strawberry or raspberry jam. Continue until batch is complete.
2. Make glacé icing by sieving icing sugar into a bowl then gradually adding a little water until a thick consistency is produced.
3. Spoon a little onto each biscuit and spread with a knife. Top with quarter glacé cherry.

Scotch Pancakes

Have ready a hot griddle over a moderate heat. Lightly grease.

200g self raising flour
3 level teaspoons baking powder
Pinch salt
25g caster sugar
1 egg
570ml milk

Makes approx 36 pancakes.

1. Sieve flour, baking powder and salt into a bowl. Add sugar.
2. Beat egg slightly and add to half of milk. Using electric whisk mix eggy milk into flour to a smooth consistency. If full 570ml of milk is used then add another egg and mix well.
3. Spoon onto heated griddle and cook for 1 min each side until golden brown.

Oatcakes

200g medium oatmeal
1 level teaspoon salt
15g dripping
water
Pinch bicarbonate of soda

1.   Add salt and bicarbonate of soda to oatmeal. Pour in melted fat.
2.   Add enough hot water to make a soft consistency. Divide in two.
3.   Knead well, working mixture into round on board sprinkled with fl
4.   Roll out into a circle as thinly as possible and cut into four. Rub w
        dry oatmeal to whiten.

Cook on a fairly hot griddle, one side only. Dry off in cool oven or under
the grill.

Scones

200g self raising flour	1 teaspoon baking powder
Pinch salt	50g margarine
1 egg yolk	Milk to mix (about 275ml)

220°C/ Gas 7
Bake – 15 minutes

1. Rub margarine into flour, baking powder, salt and sugar.
2. Add egg yolk and any flavourings.
3. Add milk until mixture is a pliable consistency but not sticky.
4. Place mixture on floured board and knead lightly. Flatten mixture by patting with your hand – do not use a rolling pin as it pushes out air from mixture.
5. Use large cutter to press out scones. Re-roll scraps and cut again. Brush with egg wash and bake in pre-heated oven. Oven must be hot or scones will not rise properly.

note: add 1 handful of sultanas at stage 2 for fruit scones.

Soda Scones

Pre-heat griddle then turn down to 2 or small flame.

500g self raising flour	Pinch salt
Milk to mix	

1. Sieve flour and salt.
2. Mix with milk until pliable consistency. Mixture should not be sticky.
3. Divide in two. Roll out to 2cm thick then cut in 4.

Place on griddle for 5-6 minutes each side.

Lemon Meringue Pie

Serve

Oven 220°C/Gas 7
7 inch (18cm) pie tin

Shortcrust pastry
100g plain flour	25g margarine
25g lard	Pinch salt
Dessertspoon caster sugar	1 egg yolk
Cold water to mix	

Filling
1 large lemon	2 tablespoons caster sugar
3 level tablespoon cornflour	2 medium egg yolks

Meringue
2 med egg whites	150g caster sugar

1. Turn on oven to pre-heat.
2. Make pastry. In mixer place flour, salt, sugar and finely chopped margarine and lard. Mix until resembles fine breadcrumbs. Add egg yolk and just enough water to bring pastry together.
3. Turn out onto floured board and roll to fit pie tin. Line pie tin with pastry, prick with a fork and bake blind for 15 minutes.
4. Filling: wash lemon, remove rind with grater and squeeze juice. Place juice and rind in measuring jug and make up to 275ml with water. Add sugar and cornflour and either thicken in a small saucepan or place jug in microwave and set for 30 seconds at a time, stirring between settings. When sauce thickens, cook for 2 minutes on low then pour into flan case.
5. Meringue: Whisk egg whites until stiff then whisk in half of sugar until stiff again. Fold in remainder of sugar then spread on top of lemon sauce. Cook at 180°C for 20 minutes or until meringue is golden brown.

Caramel Shortcake

1 batch uncooked shortbread mixture (See page 26)

400g milk chocolate

Filling:
200g margarine
100g caster sugar
400g condensed milk
1 tablespoon syrup

Oven 180ºC/Gas 5

1.   Line a Swiss roll tin with shortbread base using any leftover to make biscuits.
2.   Bake in oven for 10-15 minutes.
3.   Put all filling ingredients into a thick bottomed saucepan and bring to the boil- stir continuously or mixture will stick. Once boiling, simmer, stirring all the time for 7 minutes then pour immediately onto shortbread base.
4.   Once caramel has cooled, melt chocolate in microwave for 1 minute, stirring occasionally or until chocolate has melted.

Pour melted chocolate over caramel and leave to set. Cut into squares before chocolate has set completely.

Paradise Cake

150g margarine
150g caster sugar
150g self raising flour
Pinch salt
3 eggs
50g ground almonds
100g cherries - chopped
A few sultanas

Swiss roll tin – lined with greaseproof paper

Oven : 175ºC/ Gas 4
Bake – 30-40 mins

1.   Cream margarine and sugar.
2.   Beat in eggs.
3.   Add flour, salt, and fruit and mix until combined.
4.   Put into prepared tin.

Sprinkle ground almonds on top and bake in oven.

Meringues

This is the recipe I'm famous for. Not difficult at all.
I tend to make large shells – gives them the WOW factor.
These meringues are crisp on the outside and chewy in the middle.

For every egg white use 50g caster sugar.

6 egg whites
300g caster sugar
Pinch salt

Oven – 100ºC Gas pilot light or Gas Mark 1/2 if possible

1.   Whisk egg whites with salt in an electric mixer at room temperature.
         This will take about 4 minutes. The egg whites should be stiff and
         fluffy.   It's hard to explain the point at which to add the sugar but
         when the fluffiness just starts to come away at the sides of the bowl,
         the eggs are whisked enough.
2.   Turn mixer to low speed and add sugar, 1 tablespoon at a time but
         in quick succession. Then, turn up mixer to top speed and blitz for
         1 minute.
3.   Using a dessertspoon, place even spoonfuls of meringue onto tray,
         leaving space between each for expansion.
4.   Bake in oven for 2 hours.

Once cool, fill with whipped double cream before serving.

Banana Loaf

2x 2lb loaf tins, greased and lined with greaseproof paper

300g self raising flour
Half level teaspoon ground cinnamon
150g margarine
200g caster sugar
3 large eggs
Pinch salt
1lb ripe bananas – mashed

Oven : 180ºC/Gas 4

1. Cream margarine & sugar until white and fluffy.
2. Beat eggs into bananas and add alternatively with flour.
3. Mix until combined.

Pour mixture into prepared tins and bake for 40 – 60 mins until cooked throu

Gingerbread

2lb loaf tin, greased and lined
200g plain flour
1 teaspoon bicarbonate soda
100g margarine
1 teaspoon cinnamon
100g soft brown sugar
2 teaspoons ginger
125g black treacle
3 tablespoons milk
2 medium eggs – beaten

Oven : 150ºC / Gas 2-3

1.   Sieve dry ingredients.
2.   Melt margarine, treacle and sugar in pan. DO NOT BOIL.
3.   Add to the dry ingredients, together with eggs and milk. Beat well.
4.   Pour into prepared tin (mixture is quite runny) and bake until ready in the middle (about 1-1.5 hours). Leave to cool before cutting

Speedy Orange Cake

A quick to put-together cake for all the family.

175°C/ gas 4-5
1lb loaf tin – greased and lined with greaseproof paper
Bake 50-55 mins

125g self raising flour
100g caster sugar
75g lard
2 medium eggs
1 tablespoon orange juice
Grated rind of 1 orange

1.   Place all ingredients in mixer bowl. Switch on slowly then turn up
       speed and mix until soft and light.
2.   Fill loaf tin with mixture and bake in pre-heated oven.

Leave to cool slightly in tin before turning out onto wire rack.

Cherry Cake

8 inch (20cm) cake tin greased and lined with paper

400g self raising flour
200g margarine
150g caster sugar
4 eggs
120g glacé cherries – washed, dried and halved.

Oven : 180°C/Gas 4

1.   Cream margarine and sugar until white and fluffy.
2.   Beat eggs and add alternatively with half of flour.
3.   Toss cherries in remainder of flour.
4.   Add all this to mixture and mix in slowly.

Bake for 60 – 90 minutes until cooked through. Protect top with stiff card to stop catching.

Sultana Cake

300g caster sugar
300g margarine
8 eggs
500g sultanas
550g plain flour

175°C / Gas 4 – 1 hour
150°C / Gas 3 – 2 hours

4lb loaf tin, lined with greaseproof paper. Blind off tin by tying brown pap
round outside.

1. Cream margarine and sugar until white and fluffy.
2. Add eggs two at a time, beating thoroughly between each additio
   Add a little flour if mixture curdles.
3. Fold in flour and sultanas in 2 batches. Mix only as long as requir
   sultanas to be evenly spread through mixture.
4. Spoon into tin. Form well in centre to allow cake to rise evenly.

At end of cooking time, use a wire skewer to check if cooked. If not, repla
for another 20 mins until done.

T-Brack Fruit Loaf

200g sultanas
100g raisins
100g currants
150g Demerara sugar
250ml hot tea
1 egg
200g self raising flour

Oven 180ºC/Gas 4
Bake 40-60 minutes
This loaf freezes well.

1.   The night before, mix fruit, sugar and hot tea and steep overnight.
2.   Add all the other ingredients and beat until well mixed.
3.   Put in tin and bake.

Turn out onto wire tray and leave to cool before cutting.

Mars Bar Cake

This is great for PTA fundraisers.

100g margarine
4 mars bars
100g rice krispies

1.   Melt mars bars and margarine in microwave.
2.   Stir into rice krispies.
3.   Press into Swiss roll tin.

Cut into rectangles and leave to cool.

Egg Sponge

3 medium eggs
150g caster sugar
150g self raising flour

220°C / Gas 7
2 x 7 inch (18cm) lined sandwich pans

1.   Beat eggs and sugar until light and creamy. A spoon should leave
        thick trail.
2.   Carefully fold in flour with a metal spoon.

Divide between sandwich pans and bake for 10 minutes.

Chocolate Sponge Cake

150g margarine
150g caster sugar
3 medium eggs
150g self raising flour
1 large tablespoon cocoa powder

Icing
150g icing sugar
50g margarine
1 dessertspoon cocoa

180°C / Gas 4

1. Cream margarine and sugar until white and fluffy.
2. With mixer going add eggs, one at a time. Beat until fully mixed.
3. Add sifted flour and cocoa. Mix on low speed until incorporated.
4. Bake for 12-15 minutes.
5. Turn out and cool on baking tray before icing.

Icing – mix icing sugar, cocoa and margarine with 4 tablespoons milk and beat together until light and fluffy.

When cakes are cool, sandwich together with half the icing then use remainder to cover top. Sprinkle with grated chocolate or chocolate buttons.

Variations
Cream sponge – omit cocoa from sponge mixture. Instead of icing, sandwich with strawberry jam and whipped double cream. Dust top with icing sugar.
Coffee & Walnut – replace cocoa with 1 tablespoon instant coffee dissolved in 2 tablespoons hot water. Finely chop 50g walnuts. Mix in at stage 3.
Icing- replace cocoa with 1 tablespoon instant coffee with 3 tablespoons warm water.

KETTLEDRUM CAFÉ & BISTRO

32 EAST PRINCES STREET
ROTHESAY
TEL : 01700 505324

Located on the front street, opposite the bus and car park.

Excellent home cooking, fresh , local produce.

Fabulous baking

Open all year round.

Tablet by Trish

LUXURY SCOTTISH CONFECTIONERY

Hand Made on the Isle of Bute

available at:
Tourist Information Centre
Tofelletti Newsagent
Ettrick Bay Café
Kettledrum Café
Mountstuart

or Mail Order at : www.tabletbytrish.co.uk